Music Minus One Trumpet

12229

T0078692

Glenn Zottola

Standards for Trumpet

Getting Sentimental

- notes continued from back cover

Zottola provides a strong performance on Hoagy Carmichael's signature song **"Stardust,"** blowing the horn high and mighty on the medium tempo idiosyncratic melody making this one, the most recorded song of the 20th century. Speaking of oft-recorded standards, who can forget the 1928 George Gershwin classic **"Embraceable You,"** composed for the Broadway musical "Girl Crazy," here Zottola returns to the softer theme of the album laying down another sensuous trumpet solo perfect for the lover in as all. Sometimes referred to as one of composer Jerome Kern's most haunting melodies, **"Long Ago (and Far Away),"** was written for the 1944 Technicolor film "Cover Girl." However, there's nothing truly that haunting on this delicate version, as Zottola plays it beautifully leading the strings with one delicious solo offering after another.

There's nothing hard or boppish about *Getting Sentimental*, the music is very accessible projecting a warm and romantic mood appealing to one's softer side. Known for playing an expressive sizzling trumpet who can draw on the power of the instrument when the swing of a tune requires it, on this album, Glenn Zottola reveals himself to be more than a hot trumpeter evidenced by his graceful embrace of gentler material delivered with a solid measure of finesse and tenderness. Zottola stays true to his approach and lays down a heart-felt performance full of feeling and emotion affirming the trumpet voice as a musical messenger of love as well as an excellent interpreter of the American Songbook.

Edward Blanco
*Producer and host at WDNA, 88.9FM in Miami, Florida
as well as Critic with All About Jazz magazine*

Standards for Trumpet

Getting Sentimental

CONTENTS

©2014 MMO Music Group, Inc. All rights reserved.
ISBN 978-1-941566-92-3

MMO 12229

SOLO Bb TRUMPET

Red Sails in the Sunset

music by
Hugh Williams
lyrics by
Jimmy Kennedy

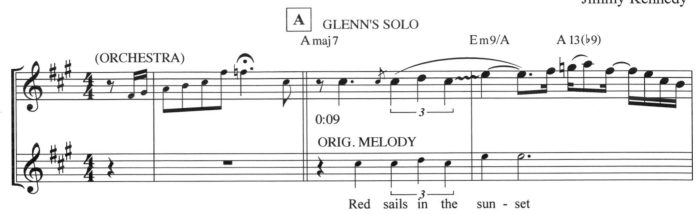

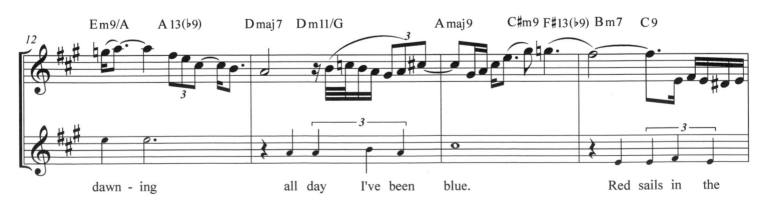

Copyright © 1935 The Peter Maurice Music Co. Ltd., London, England
Copyright Renewed and Assigned to Shapiro, Bernstein & Co., Inc., New York for U.S.A. and Canada
This arrangement Copyright © 2014 Shapiro, Bernstein & Co., Inc.
International Copyright Secured   All Rights Reserved   Used by Permission   *Reprinted by Permission of Hal Leonard Corporation*

MMO 12229

SOLO Bb TRUMPET

As Time Goes By

music and
lyrics by
Herman Hupfeld

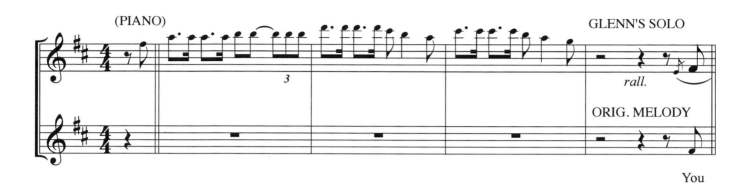

(PIANO)

GLENN'S SOLO

rall.

ORIG. MELODY

You

must re-mem-ber this, a   kiss is still a kiss, a   sigh is still a sigh;   the

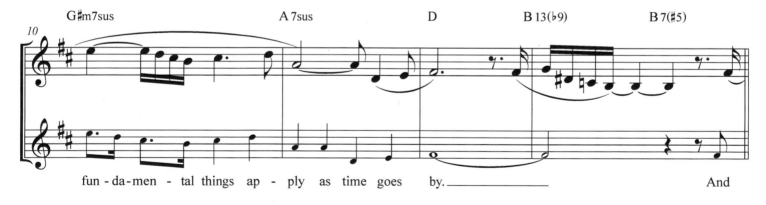

fun-da-men-tal things ap-ply as time goes   by._____   And

when two lov-ers woo,   they still say "I   love you", on   that you can   re-ly.

© 1931 (Renewed) WB MUSIC CORP.
This arrangement © 2014 WB MUSIC CORP
All Rights Reserved   Used by Permission   Reprinted by Permission of Hal Leonard Corporation

MMO 12229

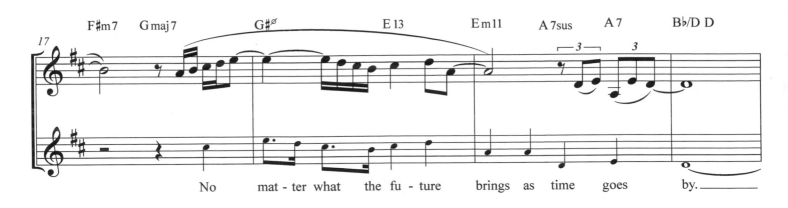

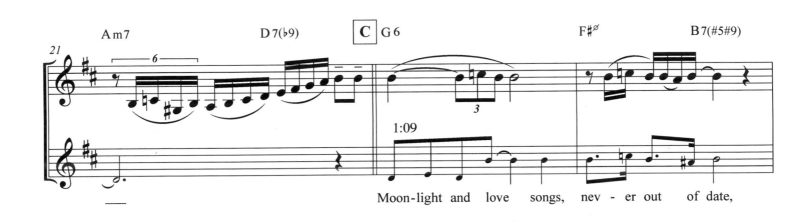

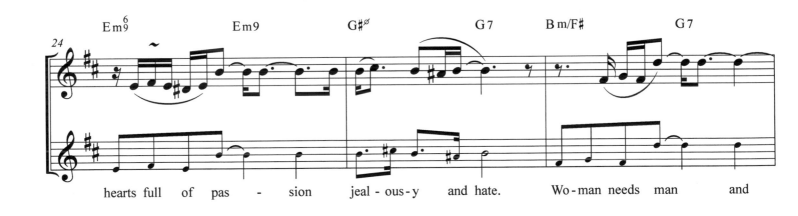

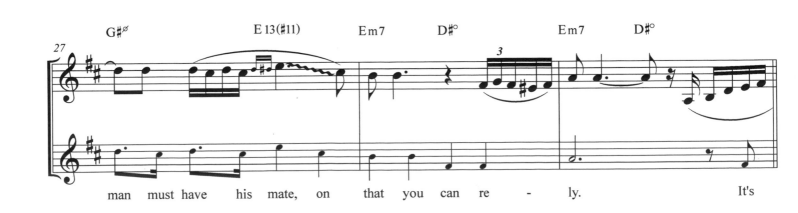

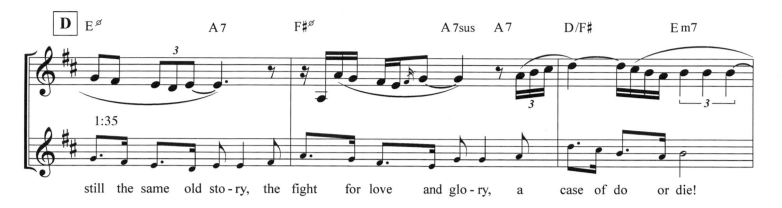

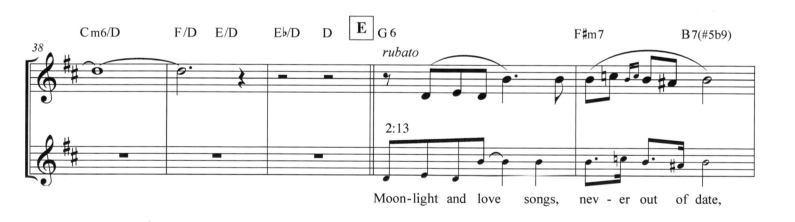

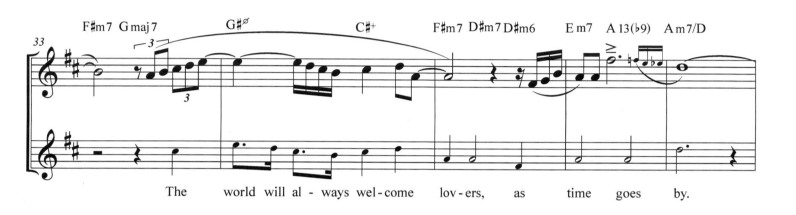

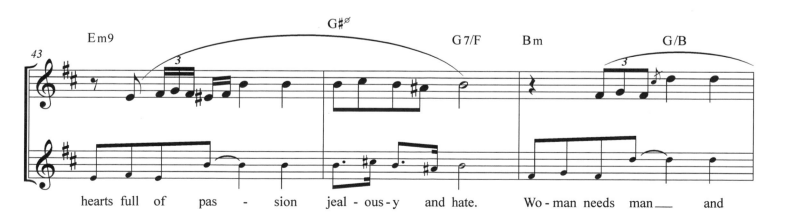

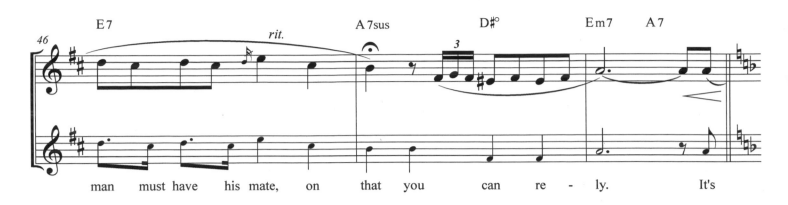

man must have his mate, on that you can re - ly. It's

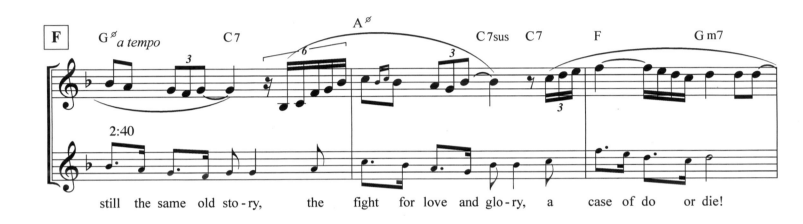

still the same old sto - ry, the fight for love and glo - ry, a case of do or die!

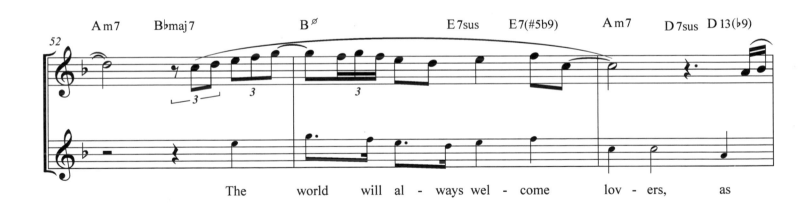

The world will al - ways wel - come lov - ers, as

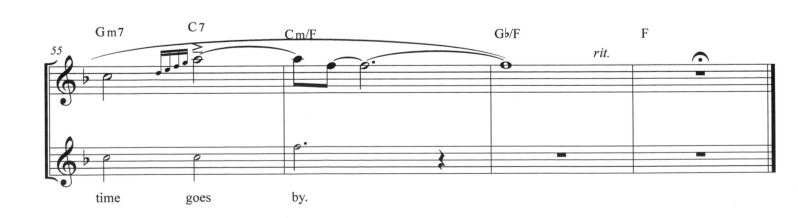

time goes by.

SOLO Bb TRUMPET

The Very Thought of You

music and lyrics by
Ray Noble

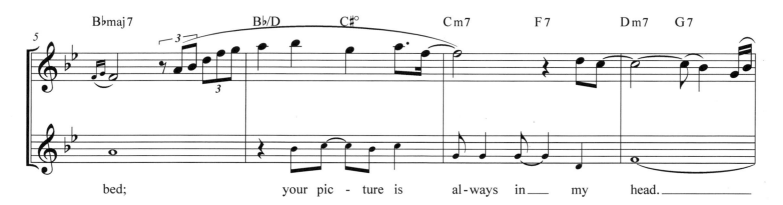

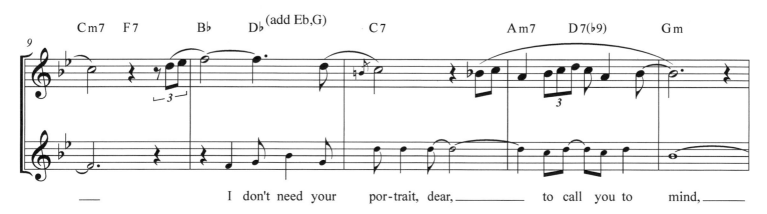

Copyright © 1934 Campbell Connelly Inc. and Warner Bros. Inc.
Copyright renewed; extended term of Copyright deriving from Ray Noble assigned and effective April 16, 1990 to Range Road Music Inc. and Quartet Music
This arrangement Copyright © 2014 Range Road Music Inc. and Quartet Music
All Rights for Quartet Music Administered by BUG Music, Inc., a BMG Chrysalis company
International Copyright Secured   All Rights Reserved   Used by Permission   Reprinted by Permission of Hal Leonard Corporation

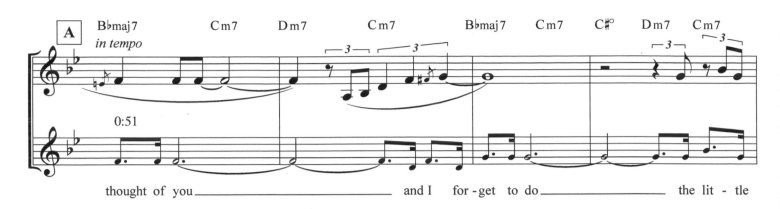

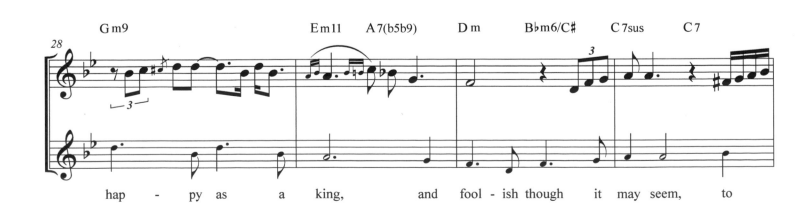

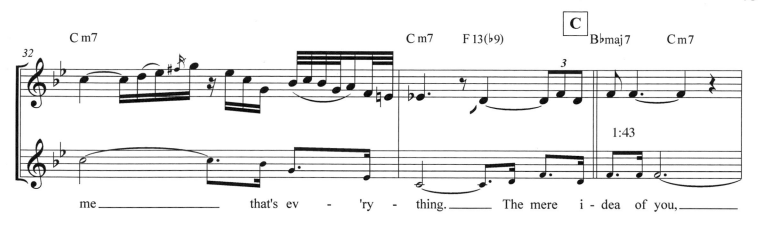

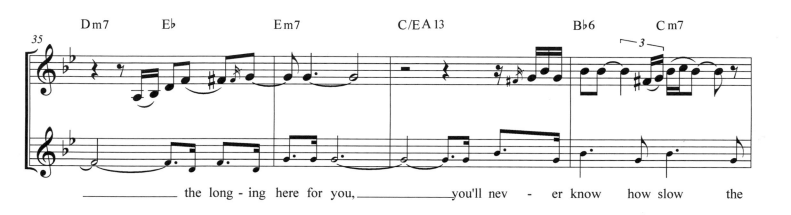

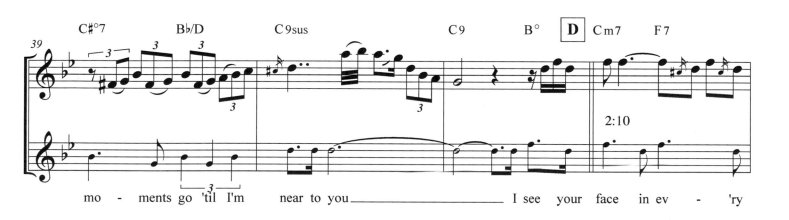

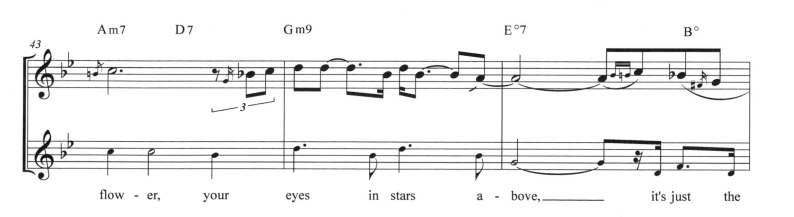

SOLO Bb TRUMPET

In The Still Of The Night

music and
lyrics by
Cole Porter

© 1937 (Renewed) WB MUSIC CORP.
This arrangement © 2014 WB MUSIC CORP
All Rights Reserved   Used by Permission   *Reprinted by Permission of Hal Leonard Corporation*

MMO 12229

SOLO Bb TRUMPET

Moonlight Becomes You

music by
Jimmy Van Heusen
lyrics by
Johnny Burke

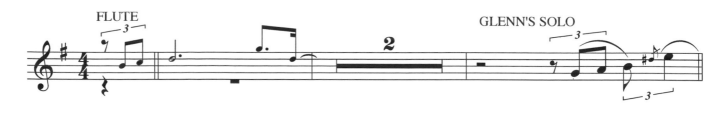

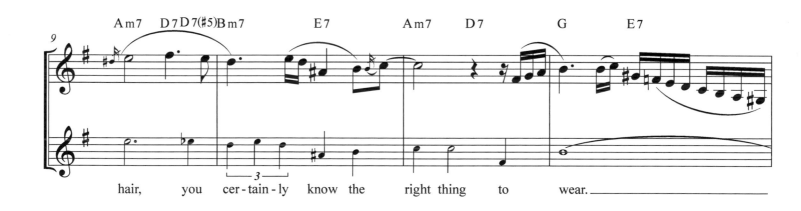

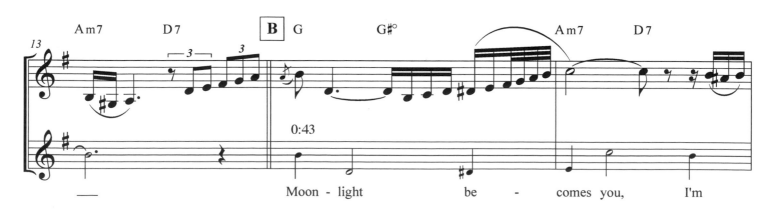

Copyright © 1942 Sony/ATV Music Publishing LLC   Copyright Renewed
This arrangement Copyright © 2014 Sony/ATV Music Publishing LLC
All Rights Administered by Sony/ATV Music Publishing LLC, 424 Church Street, Suite 1200, Nashville, TN 37219
International Copyright Secured   All Rights Reserved   Reprinted by Permission of Hal Leonard Corporation

MMO 12229

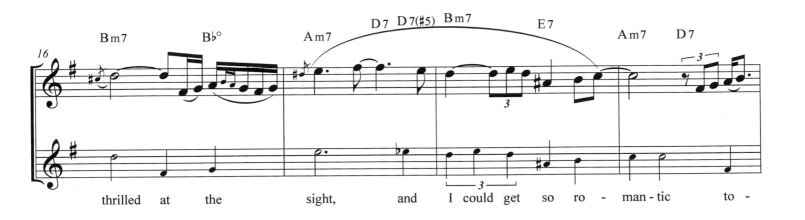

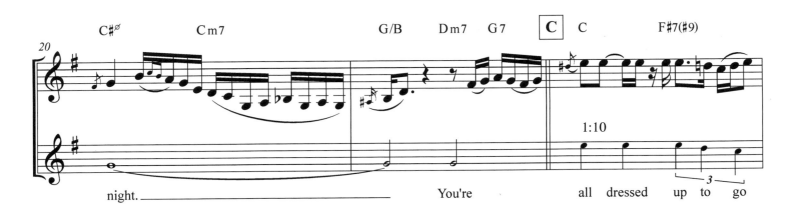

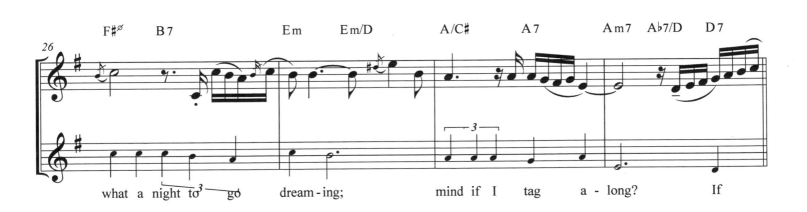

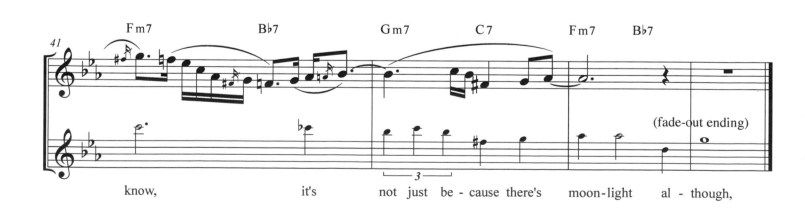

SOLO Bb TRUMPET

I'm Getting Sentimental Over You

music by
George Bassman
lyrics by
Ned Washington

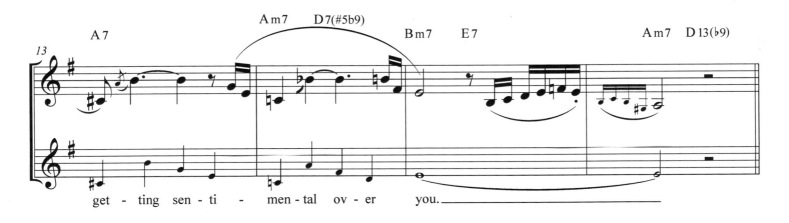

© 1932 (Renewed) EMI MILLS MUSIC INC. and CATHARINE HINEN MUSIC
This arrangement © 2014 EMI MILLS MUSIC INC. and CATHARINE HINEN MUSIC
All Rights for EMI MILLS MUSIC INC. Controlled by EMI MILLS MUSIC, INC. (Publishing) and ALFRED MUSIC (Print)
All Rights for CATHARINE HINEN MUSIC Administered by SHAPIRO, BERNSTEIN & CO., INC.
All Rights Reserved   Used by Permission   *Reprinted by Permission of Hal Leonard Corporation*

MMO 12229

get - ting sen - ti - men - tal ov - er you. _____

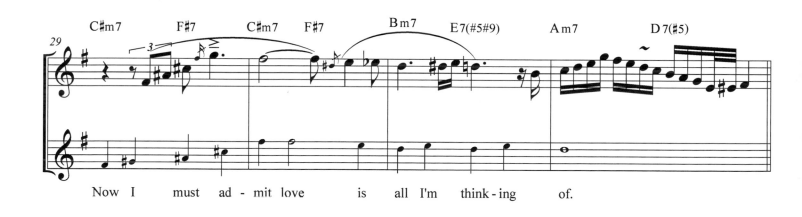

I thought I was hap - py; I could live with - out love. _____

Now I must ad - mit love is all I'm think - ing of.

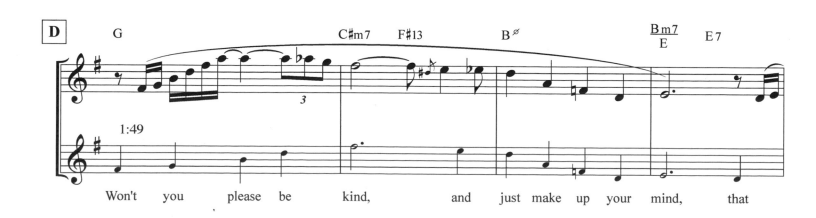

Won't you please be kind, and just make up your mind, that

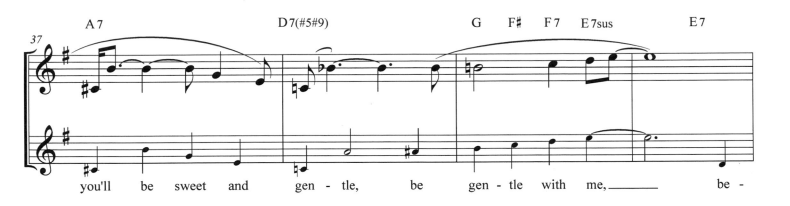

you'll be sweet and gen - tle, be gen - tle with me,_____ be -

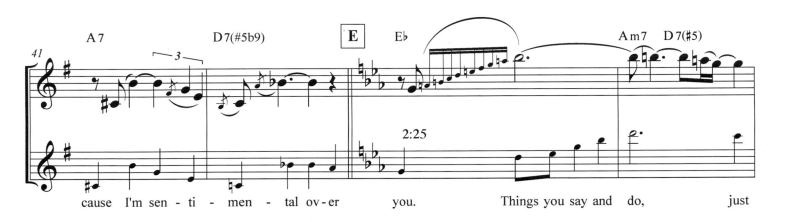

cause I'm sen - ti - men - tal ov - er you. Things you say and do, just

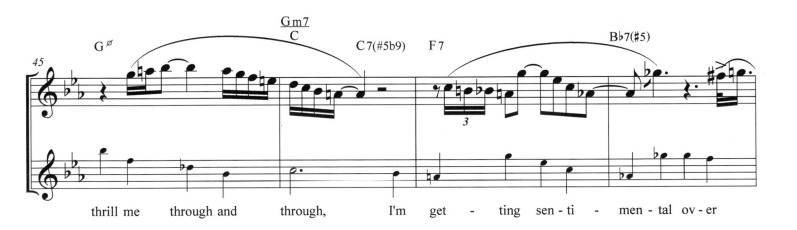

thrill me through and through, I'm get - ting sen - ti - men - tal ov - er

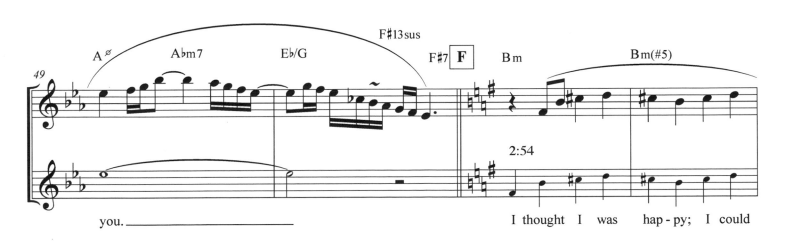

you._____ I thought I was hap - py; I could

live with - out love._____ Now I must ad - mit love is

all I'm think - ing of. Won't you please be kind, and

just make up your mind, that you'll be sweet and gen - tle, be

gen - tle with me,_____ be - cause I'm sen - ti - men - tal ov - er you.

SOLO Bb TRUMPET

Stardust

music by
Hoagy Carmichael
lyrics by
Mitchell Parish

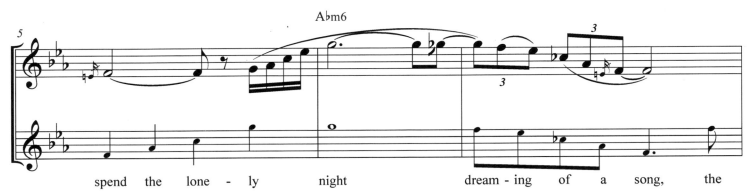

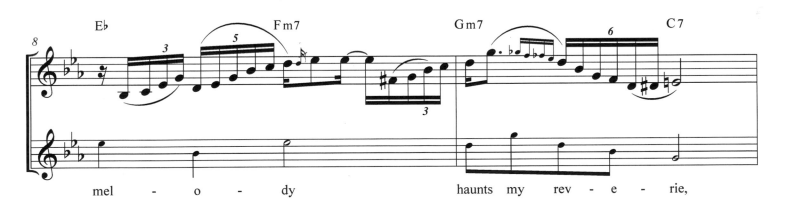

Copyright © 1928, 1929 by Songs Of Peer, Ltd. and EMI Mills Music, Inc.   Copyrights Renewed
This arrangement Copyright © 2014 by Songs Of Peer, Ltd. and EMI Mills Music, Inc.
All Rights outside the USA Controlled by EMI Mills Music, Inc. (Publishing) and Alfred Music (Print)
International Copyright Secured   All Rights Reserved   *Reprinted by Permission of Hal Leonard Corporation*

MMO 12229

and each kiss an in - spir - a - tion. _____ But

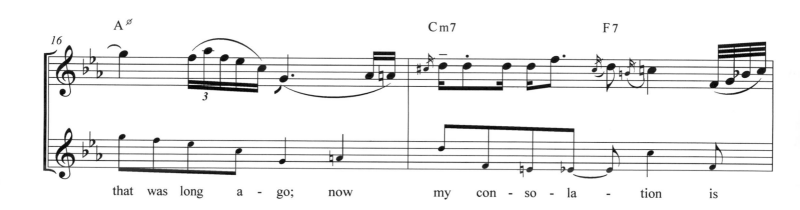

that was long a - go; now my con - so - la - tion is

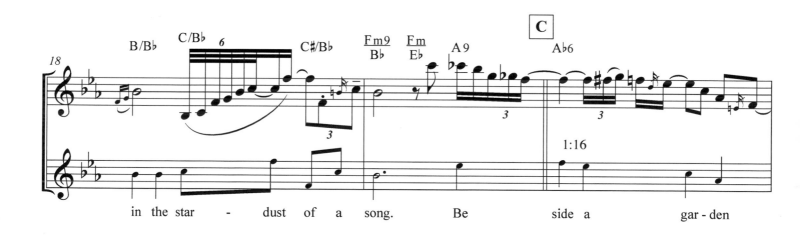

in the star - dust of a song. Be side a gar - den

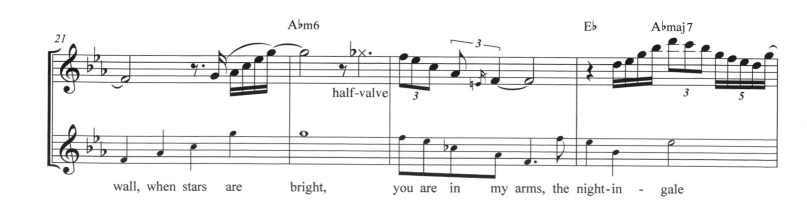

wall, when stars are bright, you are in my arms, the night-in - gale

SOLO Bb TRUMPET

Embraceable You

music by
George Gershwin
lyrics by
Ira Gershwin

© 1930 (Renewed) WB MUSIC CORP.
This arrangement © 2014 WB MUSIC CORP
All Rights Reserved   Used by Permission   *Reprinted by Permission of Hal Leonard Corporation*

MMO 12229

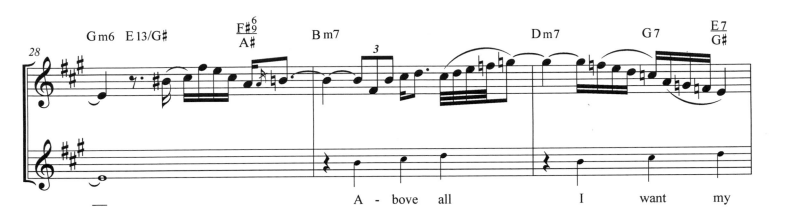

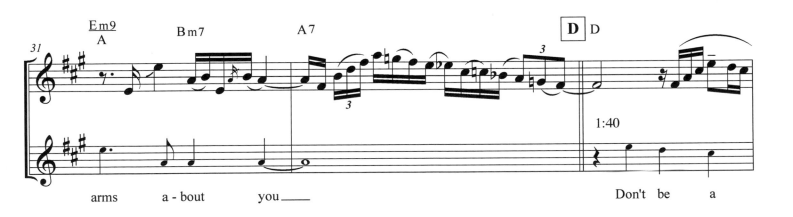

My sweet em - brace - a - ble you_____

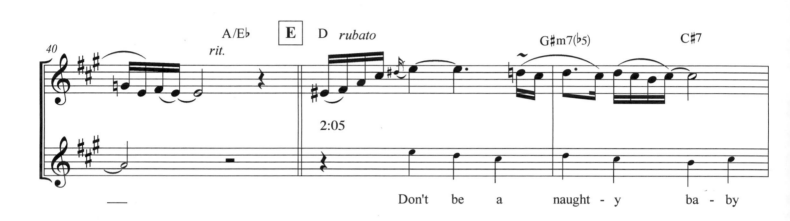

_____ Don't be a naught - y ba - by

come to pa - pa come to pa-pa do My sweet em - brace - a - ble

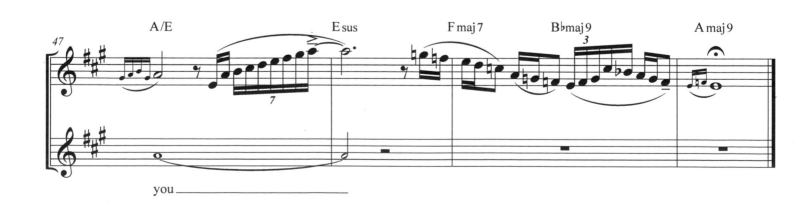

you_____

SOLO Bb TRUMPET

Long Ago and Far Away

music by
Jerome Kern
lyrics by
Ira Gershwin

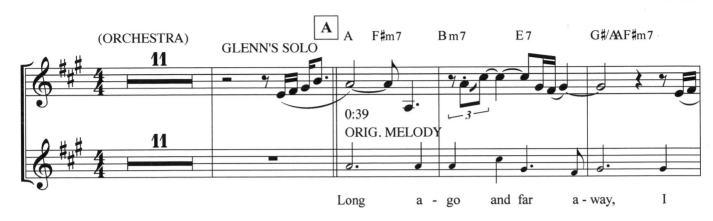

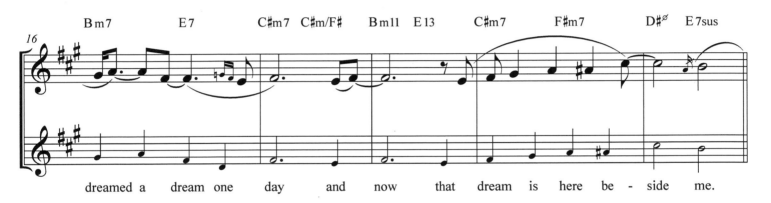

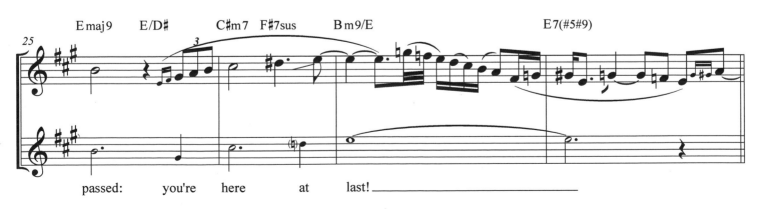

Copyright © 1944 UNIVERSAL - POLYGRAM INTERNATIONAL PUBLISHING, INC. and IRA GERSHWIN MUSIC   Copyright Renewed
This arrangement Copyright © 2014 UNIVERSAL - POLYGRAM INTERNATIONAL PUBLISHING, INC. and IRA GERSHWIN MUSIC
All Rights for IRA GERSHWIN MUSIC Administered by WB MUSIC CORP.
All Rights Reserved   Used by Permission   *Reprinted by Permission of Hal Leonard Corporation*

MMO 12229

all songs transcribed and
engraved by Mark Lopeman

MMO 12229

Music Minus One
50 Executive Boulevard • Elmsford, New York 10523-1325
914-592-1188 • e-mail: info@musicminusone.com
www.musicminusone.com

MMO 12229

ISBN 978-1-941566-92-3